JELLYFISH

Maddie Gibbs

PowerKiDS
press

New York

Published in 2014 by The Rosen Publishing Group, Inc.
29 East 21st Street, New York, NY 10010

First Edition

Editor: Amelie von Zumbusch
Book Design: Andrew Povolny

Photo Credits: Cover Andaman/Shutterstock.com; p. 5 Vilainecrevette/Shutterstock.com; p. 7 bluehand/Shutterstock.com; p. 9 Joe Drivas/Photographer's Choice/Getty Images; pp. 11, 13 iStockphoto/Thinkstock; p. 15 Stephan Kerkhofs/Shutterstock.com; p. 17 Levent Konuk/Shutterstock.com; p. 19 Edwin Verin/Shutterstock.com; p. 21 Henglein and Steets/Cultura/Getty Images; p. 23 Federic Pacorel/Photographer's Choice/Getty Images.

Library of Congress Cataloging-in-Publication Data

Gibbs, Maddie.
Jellyfish / by Maddie Gibbs. — 1st ed.
    pages cm. — (Powerkids readers: Fun fish)
Includes index.
ISBN 978-1-4777-0759-3 (library binding) — ISBN 978-1-4777-0851-4 (pbk.) —
ISBN 978-1-4777-0852-1(6-pack)
1. Jellyfishes—Juvenile literature. I. Title.
QL377.S4G53 2014
593.5'3–dc23   b839
                                        2012049069

Manufactured in the United States of America

CPSIA Compliance Information: Batch #S13PK4: For Further Information contact Rosen Publishing, New York, New York at 1-800-237-9932

Contents

Jellyfish live in seas.

4

They have for over 500 million years!

7

They are not true fish.

They have no blood, bones, or brain.

They **drift**.

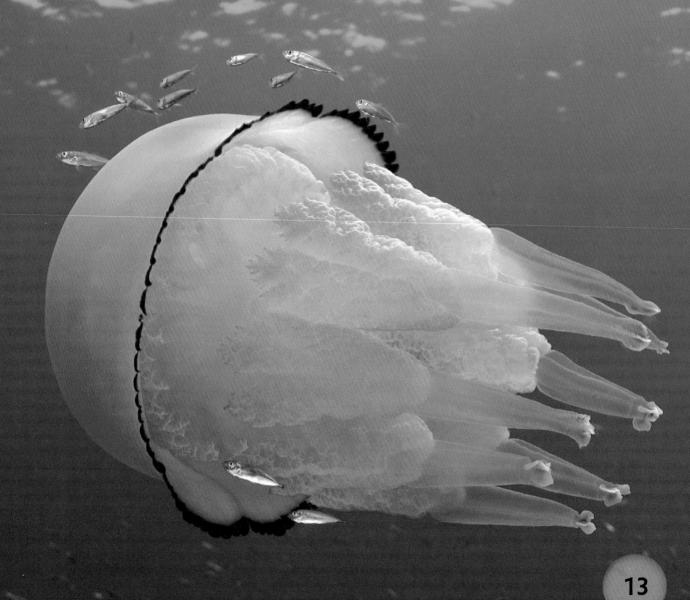

13

They are 95% water.

14

There are about 200 kinds.

A group is a **smack**.

Have you seen any?

Take care. They can sting!

WORDS TO KNOW

drift

jellyfish

smack

INDEX

WEBSITES

Due to the changing nature of Internet links, PowerKids Press has developed an online list of websites related to the subject of this book. This site is updated regularly. Please use this link to access the list:
www.powerkidslinks.com/pkrff/jelly/